Classic Christmas Carols

Jacob Cornelisz. van Amsterdam (also van Oostsanen)
Netherlandish, c. 1470–1533
Detail from *Adoration of the Christ Child*, c. 1520
Oil on panel, 98.7 x 76.5 cm.
George F. Harding Collection, 1983.375
© The Art Institute of Chicago

Classic Christmas Carols and Songs

Arrangements for Piano, Guitar, and Electronic Keyboard

BY DAN FOX

Illustrations from The Art Institute of Chicago

A Donna Martin Book

ANDREWS AND MCMEEL

A UNIVERSAL PRESS SYNDICATE COMPANY

KANSAS CITY

Title page illustration:
Jacob Cornelisz. van Amsterdam (also van Oostsanen)
Netherlandish, c. 1470–1533
Detail from *Adoration of the Christ Child,* c. 1520
Oil on panel, 98.7 x 76.5 cm
George F. Harding Collection, 1983.375
© The Art Institute of Chicago

Classic Christmas Carols and Songs arrangements and commentary copyright © 1994 by Dan Fox.
Illustrations copyright © 1994 by The Art Institute of Chicago.
Designed by Irene Wallace.
All rights reserved. Printed in Singapore. No part of this book may be used or reproduced in any manner whatsoever
except in the case of reprints in the context of reviews. For information write
Andrews and McMeel
A Universal Press Syndicate Company,
4900 Main Street, Kansas City, Missouri 64112.

Library of Congress Cataloging-in-Publication Data
Classic Christmas carols and songs / arrangements for piano, guitar, and electronic keyboard by Dan Fox.
p.   cm.
For voice and piano/guitar/electronic keyboard; includes chord symbols.
"A Donna Martin book."
"Illustrations from the Art Institute of Chicago."
Includes index.
ISBN 0-8362-4514-8 : $14.95
1. Carols, English. 2. Songs with piano. 3. Christmas music.
I. Fox, Dan. II. Art Institute of Chicago.
M1629.3.C5C618   1994   94-24876
CIP
M

Contents

Jacob Cornelisz. van Amsterdam
(also van Oostsanen)
Netherlandish, c. 1470–1533
Detail from *Adoration of the Christ Child*, c. 1520
Oil on panel, 98.7 x 76.5 cm.
George F. Harding Collection, 1983.375
© The Art Institute of Chicago

Foreword

WHAT FAMOUS CHRISTMAS HYMN was written to celebrate the invention of the printing press? Why would "Silent Night" have never been written if it hadn't been for mice? What famous Christmas song was written for Thanksgiving? What beautiful carol started out as a bawdy Elizabethan ballad?

You'll learn the answers to these fascinating bits of Christmas lore and you'll discover the stories behind many other carols and hymns in this book. They are presented here in easy arrangements for piano and voice by one of America's best known music arrangers, Dan Fox. Although the songs are playable by pianists of very limited skills, they sound rich and full and are packed with interesting musical twists and turns. They can be played on electronic keyboards, too, and there are chord symbols for guitarists and those keyboard players who prefer to create their own arrangements. Singers will be pleased to note that all the words to these beloved songs are included.

This fine collection is graced by the inclusion of masterpieces from the Art Institute of Chicago in full-color reproductions.

You'll return to this book at every season for the beauty of its art, its interesting anecdotes, and the simplicity and professional sound of its arrangements.

Lucas van Leyden (follower of)
Netherlandish, 1494–1538
The Adoration of the Magi, c. 1510
Oil on cradled panel, 28.7 x 35.7 cm.
Mr. and Mrs. Martin A. Ryerson Collection, 1933.1045
© The Art Institute of Chicago

Adeste Fideles

(O COME ALL YE FAITHFUL)

English words by Frederick Oakeley
Latin words by John Francis Wade

Music by John Francis Wade

JOHN FRANCIS WADE was an Englishman who lived and worked in France in the eighteenth century. He seems to have been the author of both the Latin words and the music of this beloved hymn. Yet some authorities believe the melody is much older, a Latin carol meant to be danced around the crèche during a Christmas play. (The word "carol" originally meant a round or circle dance with singing.) One of the earliest American editions dates from 1803 and bears the curious subtitle: "The favorite Portuguez [sic] Hymn on the Nativity." No one knows why. The English words were written in 1852 by Frederick Oakeley, a Catholic priest who eventually became Canon of Westminster in London.

Ad - es - te fi - de - les, lae - ti tri - um - phan - tes; ve - ni - te, ve -
O come, all ye faith - ful, joy - ful and tri - um - phant, O come ye, O

ni - te in Beth - le - hem. Na - tum vi - de - te,
come ye to Beth - le - hem. Come and be - hold Him,

Re - gem an - ge - lo - rum. Ve - ni - te ad - o - re - mus, ve - ni - te ad - o -
Born the King of an - gels. O come let us a - dore Him, O come let us a -

re - mus, ve - ni - te ad - o - re - mus ___ Do - mi - num.
dore Him, O come let us a - dore Him, ___ Christ ___ the Lord.

2. Sing, choirs of angels, sing in exultation,
   Sing all ye citizens of heav'n above:
   Glory to God, in the highest:
   O come let us adore Him,
   O come let us adore Him,
   O come let us adore Him, Christ the Lord.

3. Yea, Lord, we greet Thee, born this happy morning,
   Jesus, to Thee be glory giv'n;
   Word of the Father
   Now in flesh appearing:
   O come let us adore Him,
   O come let us adore Him,
   O come let us adore Him, Christ the Lord.

I Saw Three Ships

Traditional

THE BIBLE MAKES no mention of the Virgin Mary or Jesus ever having set foot on a ship. And, of course, Bethlehem is nowhere near the Mediterranean. Nevertheless, this carol depicting Mary and Jesus on a ship has been sung for over three hundred years. It is as popular as ever.

Folk song authority Cecil Sharp speculates that this British carol is about ships because that's what Britons are familiar with. Because Britain is an island, many of its people depend on the sea for their livelihood.

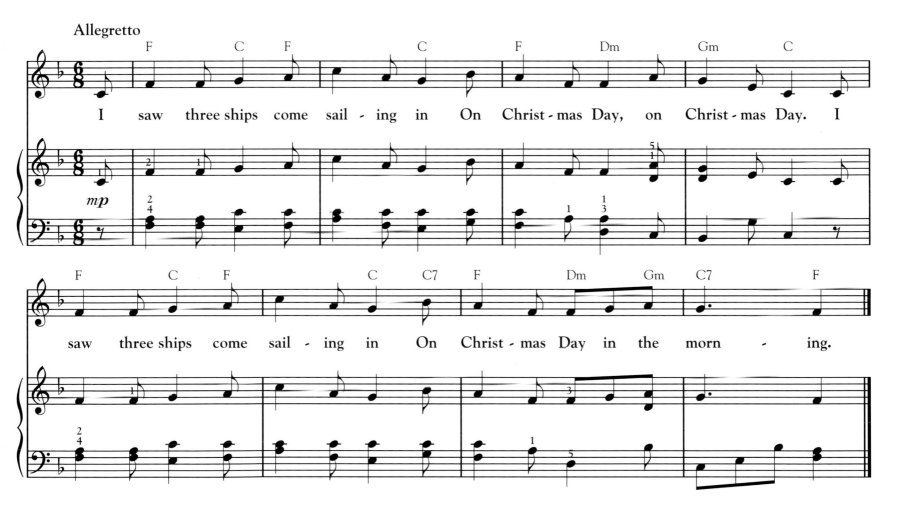

2. And what was in those ships all three,
On Christmas Day, on Christmas Day?
And what was in those ships all three
On Christmas Day in the morning?

(continue similarly)

3. Our Savior Christ and His Lady . . .

4. Pray, whither sailed those ships all three? . . .

5. O, they sailed into Bethlehem . . .

6. And all the bells on earth shall ring . . .

7. And all the angels in Heav'n shall sing . . .

8. And all the souls on earth shall sing . . .

9. Then let us all rejoice amain . . .

O Little Town Of Bethlehem

Words by Phillips Brooks

Music by Lewis H. Redner

In December of 1865 Phillips Brooks, a thirty-year-old Philadelphia minister was in the Holy Land in Jerusalem. On Christmas Eve he traveled on horseback to Bethlehem to visit the site where the shepherds had been when they saw the Star. Brooks was deeply moved by the experience, and three years later he wrote the words for "O Little Town of Bethlehem," intending it as a children's hymn.

He gave his poem to Lewis Redner, the church organist, who composed the lovely melody just in time for Christmas in 1868. The hymn was well received but did not attain wide popularity until it was included in the Episcopal Hymnal of 1892. Phillips Brooks lived from 1835 to 1893; Lewis Redner from 1831 to 1908.

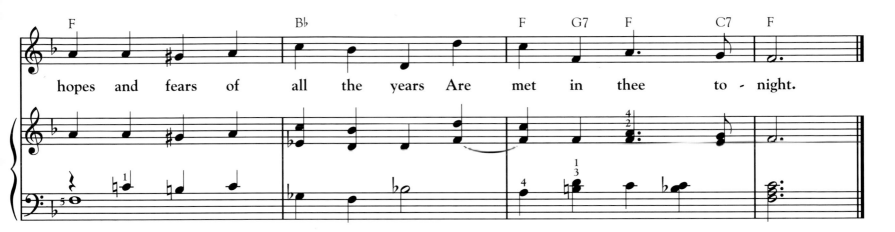

hopes and fears of all the years Are met in thee to - night.

2. For Christ is born of Mary, And gathered all above,
    While mortals sleep, the angels keep Their watch of wondering love.
    O morning stars, together Proclaim the holy birth!
    And praises sing to God the King, And peace to men on earth.

3. How silently, how silently, The wondrous gift is giv'n!
    So God imparts to human hearts The blessings of his heav'n.
    No ear may hear his coming, But in this world of sin,
    Where meek souls will receive him, still The dear Christ enters in.

4. Where children pure and happy Pray to the blessed Child,
    Where misery cries out to Thee, Son of the mother mild;
    Where charity stands watching And faith holds wide the door,
    The dark night wakes, the glory breaks, And Christmas comes once more.

5. O holy Child of Bethlehem! Descend to us, we pray;
    Cast out our sin and enter in, Be born in us today.
    We hear the Christmas angels The great glad tidings tell;
    O come to us, abide with us, Our Lord, Immanuel.

Briton Riviere
English, 1840–1920
Star of Bethlehem
Lithograph, 25.4 x 61 cm.
Bequest of Kate S. Buckingham, 1938.718
© The Art Institute of Chicago

What Child Is This?

Words by William Chatterton Dix

Music: Anonymous

PEOPLE HAVE BEEN singing, playing, and dancing to the song "Greensleeves" for over four hundred years. In fact, Shakespeare knew the melody. In *The Merry Wives of Windsor* Falstaff declaims, "Let the sky . . . thunder to the tune of Greensleeves."

The original words of "Greensleeves" were not very respectable. Many other lyrics have been sung to this melody, among them a 1642 carol called "The Old Year Now Away Has Fled." In Shakespeare's day the song was played at a rather fast tempo for dancing, but the real beauty of the melody was revealed when someone had the idea of playing it much more slowly. In 1865 English insurance man and sometime poet William Chatterton Dix wrote these words to be sung to the slower version. Dix was also the author of another famous Christmas hymn, "As With Gladness Men of Old," (p.34) supposedly written on the same day as "What Child Is This?"

This this is Christ the King, Whom shep-herds guard and an-gels sing:

Haste, haste to bring Him laud, The Babe, the Son of Mar-y.

2. Why lies He in such mean estate,
   Where ox and ass are feeding?
   Good Christian, fear, for sinners here
   The silent word is pleading.

   Nails, spear, shall pierce Him through,
   The Cross be borne for me, for you:
   Hail, hail, the Word made flesh,
   The Babe, the Son of Mary.

3. So bring Him incense, gold, and myrrh,
   Come peasant, king, to own Him.
   The King of Kings salvation brings;
   Let loving hearts enthrone Him.

   Raise, raise the song on high,
   The Virgin sings her lullaby:
   Joy, joy, for Christ is born,
   The Babe, the son of Mary.

God Rest Ye Merry, Gentlemen

Traditional

THE CAROL IS VERY OLD. The word "ye" in the title is an archaic form of "you." The word "rest" used this way means "keep." So the title really means "(May) God keep you merry, gentlemen." The music, too, seems to come from an earlier time when modes* were used instead of scales.

In Charles Dickens's *A Christmas Carol* Scrooge gets angry when he hears this cheerful carol sung in the street. The song, first published in its complete form in 1827, was well known in Dickens's London where groups of carol singers strolled the streets during the holiday season.

Joyously

God rest ye mer - ry, gen - tle - men, Let noth - ing you dis - may. Re -

mem - ber Christ our Sav - ior Was born on Christ - mas day; To

save us all from Sa - tan's pow'r When we were gone a - stray:

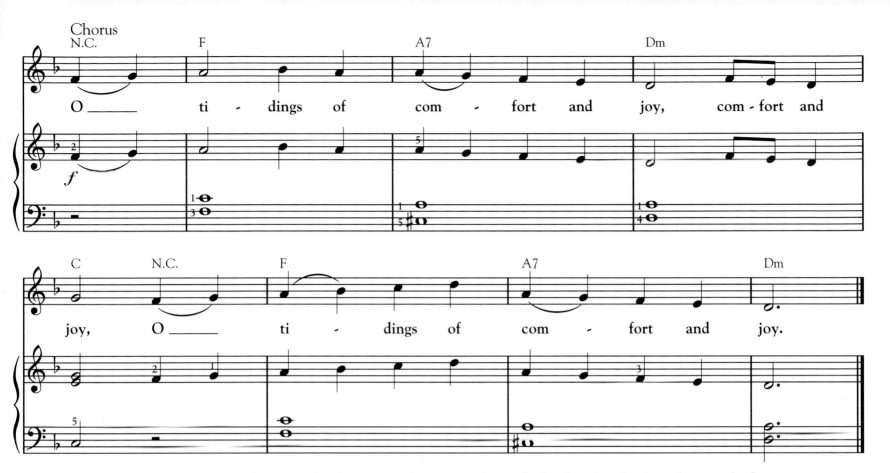

*Modes are ancient forms of scales originally used in church music. On the piano, modes can be found on the white keys. For example, the notes D E F G A B C D are called the Dorian mode; the notes E F G A B C D E are called the Phrygian mode, and so on.

2. In Bethlehem in Jewry
   This blessèd Babe was born,
   And laid within a manger
   Upon this blessèd morn;
   The which His mother Mary
   Did nothing take in scorn:
        (repeat Chorus after each verse)

3. From God our heavenly Father
   A blesséd angel came,
   And unto certain shepherds
   Brought tidings of the same,
   How that in Bethlehem was born
   The Son of God by name:

4. "Fear not," then said the angel,
   "Let nothing you affright,
   This day is born a Savior
   Of a pure Virgin bright,
   To free all those who trust in Him
   From Satan's power and might,"

5. The shepherds at those tidings
   Rejoicèd much in mind,
   And left their flocks a-feeding
   In tempest, storm and wind,
   And went to Bethlehem straightway
   This blessèd Babe to find:

6. But when to Bethlehem they came,
   Whereat this Infant lay,
   They found Him in a manger,
   Where oxen feed on hay;
   His Mother Mary kneeling,
   Unto the Lord did pray:

7. Now to the Lord sing praises,
   All you within this place,
   And with true love and brotherhood
   Each other now embrace;
   This holy tide of Christmas
   All others doth deface;

Desmond Chute
English
Virgin and Child
Woodcut 7 x 9 6

The Cherry Tree Carol

Traditional

THE ORIGINAL "Cherry Tree Carol" tells of a miracle when Christ was yet unborn. Mary and Joseph were walking in an orchard. When Joseph refused to pick a cherry that Mary had asked for, the tree bent over to give her the fruit.

There is no biblical source for this story; the first mention of it dates from the fifteenth century. The words printed here are from a much later date.

As Jo - seph was a - walk - ing, He heard an an - gel sing, "This night shall be the birth - time Of ___ Christ, the ___ Heav'n-ly King."

2. He neither shall be born
   In housen nor in hall,
   Nor in the place of paradise,
   But in an ox's stall.

3. He neither shall be clothed
   In purple nor in pall,
   But in the fair white linen
   That usen babies all.

4. He neither shall be rocked
   In silver nor in gold,
   But in a wooden manger
   That resteth on the mould.

O Sanctissima

Traditional

IN THE 1960s the civil rights movement in the United States won many victories for disadvantaged groups, especially African Americans. The most famous song of the movement was a hymn called "We Shall Overcome." This stirring anthem was originally called "The Sicilian Mariner's Hymn," first published in the late eighteenth century with the Latin words printed below. No one knows the origins of the melody, whether it really is Sicilian, or even who wrote these English words. The words of "We Shall Overcome" were written in 1960 by a group of four songwriters, including folksinger Pete Seeger.

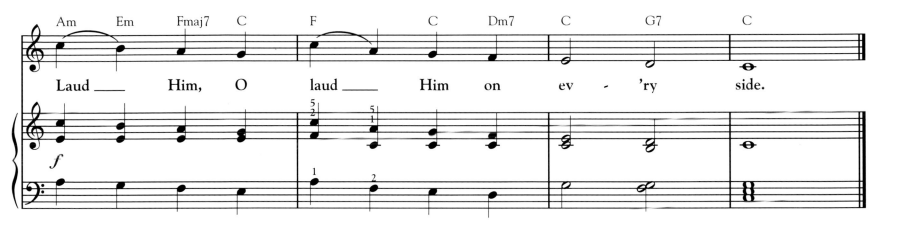

Laud ___ Him, O laud ___ Him on ev - 'ry side.

2. O thou joyful day,
O thou blessed day,
Holy peaceful Christmastide.
King of glory,
We bow before Thee,
Laud Him, O laud Him
On every side.

(original Latin words)
O sanctissima,
O piissima,
Dulcis Virgo Maria.
Mater amata, intemerata,
Ora, ora pro nobis.

Panel from American
Album Quilt, 1845–1850
Cotton appliqued, embroidered and quilted, 228 x 229.5 cm.
Mrs. Chauncey B. Borland, 1957.524
© The Art Institute of Chicago

Auld Lang Syne

Words by Robert Burns

Music: Anonymous

Iɴ ᴛʜᴇ 1920s radio became very popular. By the end of the twenties most American families had a radio which, like TV today, was the focus of evenings at home. At midnight on the last day of 1929 the popular orchestra of Guy Lombardo and his Royal Canadians broadcast their tremulous arrangement of "Auld Lang Syne," and from that time to this the tune has been associated with New Year's Eve. Although the famous Scottish poet Robert Burns is credited with the words, scholars believe that the first and best-known verse is not by him. "Auld Lang Syne" translates as "old times' sake."

*Guitarists: Place capo on 3rd fret and use chord symbols in parentheses.

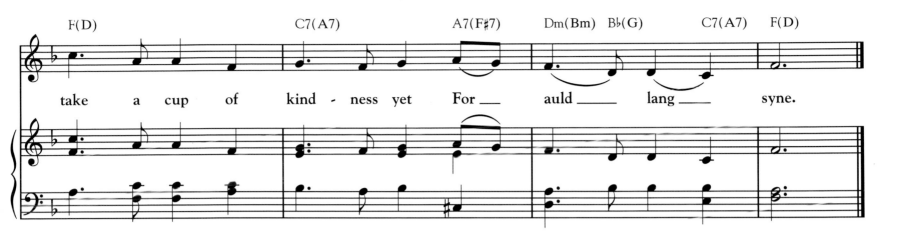

| F(D) | C7(A7) | A7(F♯7) | Dm(Bm) | B♭(G) | C7(A7) | F(D) |

take   a   cup   of   kind - ness   yet   For ___   auld ___   lang ___   syne.

2. And here's a hand, my trusty friend,
   And gives a hand o' thine,
   We'll take a cup o' kindness yet
   For auld lang syne.
   For auld lang syne, my dear,
   For auld lang syne,
   We'll take a cup of kindness yet,
   For auld lang syne.

George Hunt, after James Pollard (English)
Approach to Christmas, c. 1825
Aquatint, 38 x 52 cm.
Given in memory of Charles Netcher, 1925.294
© The Art Institute of Chicago

The First Noël

Traditional

Noël is the French word for Christmas. On *la nuit avant Noël* (the night before Christmas) French children wait for *Bonhomme Noël* (Santa Claus), who leaves toys and sweets on the hearth for the children who have been good.

But if they have been naughty, the bogeyman, *Père Fouettard* comes instead and leaves a bundle of switches to spank them. The first complete version of this carol in English dates from 1833.

cold win - ter's night _____ that was _____ so deep.

Chorus

No - ël, _____ No - ël, No - ël, No - ël,

Born is the King _____ of Is - ra - el.

2. They looked up and saw a star,
   Shining in the East beyond them far;
   And to the earth it gave great light,
   And so it continued day and night.
        (repeat Chorus)

3. This star drew nigh to the northwest;
   O'er Bethlehem it took its rest,
   And there it did both stop and stay,
   Right o'er the place where Jesus lay.
        (repeat Chorus)

4. Then entered in there Wise Men three,
   Fall rev'rently upon their knee,
   And offered there in His presence
   Their gold and myrrh and frankincense.
        (repeat Chorus)

The Friendly Beasts

Traditional

IN THIS CHARMING twelfth-century English carol, every animal in the stable has a special task: The donkey has brought Mary to Bethlehem; the cow has given up its manger for the baby Jesus; the sheep has given its wool for a blanket; the dove coos the baby to sleep; and even the stubborn, bad-tempered camel has carried the Wise Men to worship the infant.

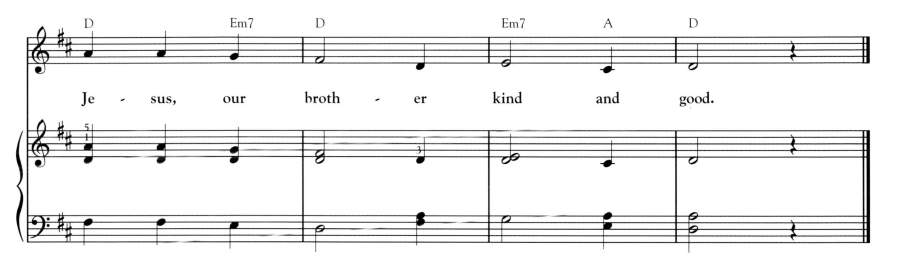

Je - sus, our broth - er kind and good.

2. "I," said the donkey, shaggy and brown,
   "I carried His mother up hill and down;
   I carried her safely to Bethlehem town."
   "I," said the donkey, shaggy and brown.

3. "I," said the cow, all white and red,
   "I gave Him my manger for a bed;
   I gave Him my hay to pillow His head."
   "I," said the cow, all white and red.

4. "I," said the sheep with curly horn,
   "I gave Him my wool for His blanket warm;
   He wore my coat on Christmas morn."
   "I," said the sheep with curly horn.

5. "I," said the dove from the rafters high,
   "Cooed Him to sleep that He should not cry;
   We cooed Him to sleep, my mate and I."
   "I," said the dove from the rafters high.

6. "I," said the camel, yellow and black,
   "Over the desert, upon my back,
   I brought Him a gift in the Wise Men's pack."
   "I," said the camel, yellow and black.

7. Thus every beast by some good spell,
   In the stable dark was glad to tell
   Of the gift he gave Emmanuel,
   The gift he gave Emmanuel.

Eric Gill
English, 1881–1940
Animals All, 1920
Woodblock print, 5.5 x 5.5 cm.
Gift of the Print and Drawing Club, 1924.2.28
© The Art Institute of Chicago

Bring A Torch, Jeanette Isabella

Traditional

ALTHOUGH SCHOLARS don't know who wrote this charming carol, we do know that the music comes from a fourteenth-century French court dance called a *ritournelle*. The words are a translation of those that appeared in a sixteenth-century French collection of Christmas music; they tell us how exciting the very first Christmas must have been.

2. Hasten now, good folk of the village;
   Hasten now, the Christ Child to see.
   You will find Him asleep in the manger;
   Quietly come and whisper softly:
   Hush, hush, peacefully now He slumbers;
   Hush, hush, peacefully now He sleeps.

The Holly And The Ivy

Traditional

ROMAN LEGIONS under the command of Julius Caesar conquered Britain in 55 B.C. This was the beginning of an occupation that lasted over four hundred years. The early Britons adopted many Roman customs, including a feast called the *Saturnalia* that took place on or about the winter solstice in late December. Like the Romans, the Britons decorated their homes with holly, ivy, and other evergreens. The early Christians, in turn, took over this custom which has lasted to the present day.

The holly was thought to give special meaning to the life of Christ. The pointed leaves symbolized the crown of thorns, and the red berries suggested his blood. Because of its pagan origins, holly was for a period banned from Christmas celebrations in most of Europe. But because it remained so popular in England, the Church ultimately accepted it.

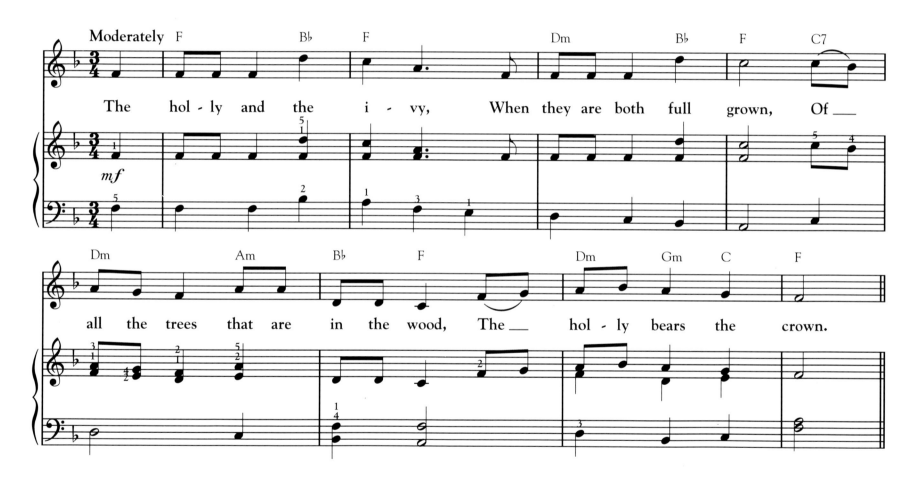

The hol-ly and the i-vy, When they are both full grown, Of all the trees that are in the wood, The hol-ly bears the crown.

Chorus

The ris-ing of the sun, And the run-ning of the deer, The play-ing of the mer-ry or-gan, Sweet sing-ing of the choir.

2. The holly bears a blossom
As white as lily flower;
And Mary bore sweet Jesus Christ
To be our sweet Savior.
   (repeat Chorus)

3. The holly bears a berry
As red as any blood;
And Mary bore sweet Jesus Christ
To do poor sinners good.
   (repeat Chorus)

4. The holly bears a prickle
As sharp as any thorn;
And Mary bore sweet Jesus Christ
On Christmas Day in the morn.
   (repeat Chorus)

5. The holly and the ivy,
When they are both full-grown,
Of all the trees that are in the wood,
The holly bears the crown.
   (repeat Chorus)

I Know A Rose Tree Springing

(Lo, How a Rose E'er Blooming)

Traditional

HUNDREDS OF YEARS before the birth of Jesus the rose was associated with Aphrodite, the Greek goddess of love. Supposedly her son Cupid was stung by a bee when he stopped to smell a rose. Enraged, he shot an arrow into the bush, which is how the rose acquired its thorns. But, according to a fourth-century bishop, the rose was thornless until it was expelled from the Garden of Eden.

During the Middle Ages many Christian cults sprang up that worshiped the Virgin Mary. Gradually some cults assigned to her attributes of the rose, especially as a symbol of perfect love. In this serene 1599 German carol, Mary is the rose tree or bush, and Jesus is her blossom.

Performance note: There are many changes of meter in this carol, but throughout the quarter note is played at a steady beat of about ♩ = 100.

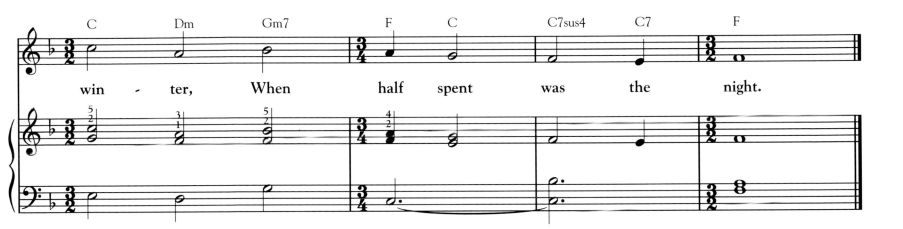

win - ter, When half spent was the night.

2. This rose-tree, blossom laden,
   Whereof Isaiah spake
   Is Mary, spotless Maiden,
   Who mothered, for our sake,
   The little Child, newborn
   By God's eternal counsel
   On that first Christmas morn.

3. O Flow'r, whose fragrance tender
   With sweetness fills the air,
   Dispel in glorious splendor
   The darkness ev'rywhere;
   True man, yet very God,
   From sin and death now save us,
   And share our ev'ry load.

Panel from American
Album Quilt, 1845–1850
Cotton appliqued, embroidered
and quilted, 228 x 229.5 cm.
Mrs. Chauncey B. Borland, 1957.524
© The Art Institute of Chicago

As With Gladness Men Of Old

Words by William Chatterton Dix

Music by Conrad Kocher

ACCORDING TO LEGEND William Chatterton Dix wrote this and his other famous carol, "What Child Is This?" on a single day in 1859. Because the Gospels do not mention "Wise Men," "Magi," or "Kings," Dix decided to call them simply "men."

Still, some modern historians believe there were "Wise Men," or astrologers (astronomers, really), who came from Mesopotamia, which is present-day Iraq. They would have noticed any unusual events in the night sky. Such an event took place in 7 B.C. when Saturn, Mars, and Jupiter appeared very close together in the constellation of Pisces. (Because of revisions in the calendar, historians now believe that Jesus was born seven years before the beginning of the Christian era.) Ordinary people would not have given this phenomenon much note, but astrologers would have found it significant, perhaps important enough to merit a long and difficult journey. Perhaps this coincidence of planets was the "star" that led the Wise Men to Bethlehem.

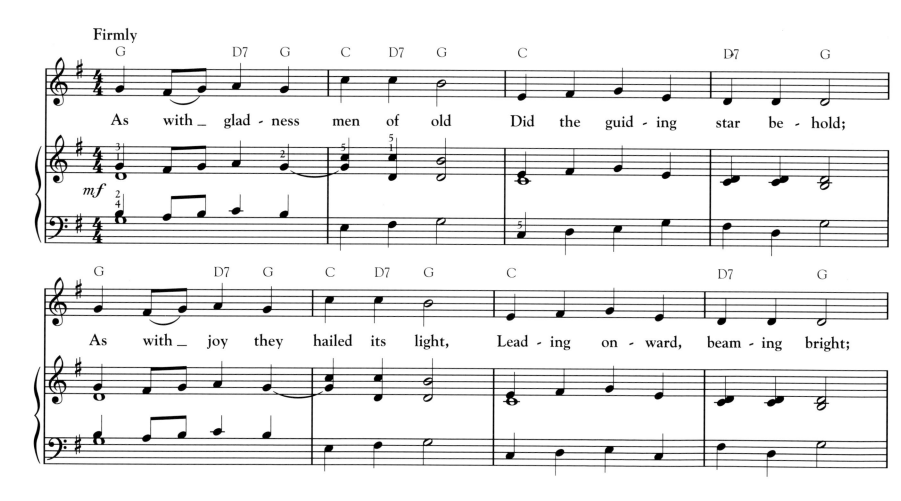

As with gladness men of old Did the guid-ing star be-hold;

As with joy they hailed its light, Lead-ing on-ward, beam-ing bright;

So, most gra - cious Lord, may we   Ev - er - more be   led to Thee.

2. As with joyful steps they sped
   To that lowly manger bed,
   There to bend the knee before
   Him whom heaven and earth adore;
   So may we with willing feet
   Ever seek thy mercy-seat.

3. As they offered gifts most rare
   At that manger rude and bare;
   So may we with holy joy,
   Pure and free from sin's alloy,
   All our costliest treasures bring,
   Christ, to Thee, our heavenly King.

4. Holy Jesus, every day
   Keep us in the narrow way;
   And, when earthly things are past,
   Bring our ransomed souls at last
   Where they need no star to guide,
   Where no clouds thy glory hide.

5. In the heavenly country bright,
   Need they no created light;
   Thou its light, its joy, its crown,
   Thou its sun which goes not down;
   There forever may we sing
   Alleluias to our King.

Fröhliche Weihnachten

Gustave Baumann
American, 1881–1971
Fröhliche Weihnachten
Linoleum cut, 33 x 24.8 cm.
Gift of Mrs. W. G. Hibbard, 1923.524
© The Art Institute of Chicago

Silent Night

*English words adapted from
the German of Joseph Mohr*

Music by Franz Gruber

J UST BEFORE CHRISTMAS IN 1818, an Austrian village priest named Father Joseph Mohr noticed that the church organ had been damaged by mice and could not be played. Needing something to sing on Christmas Eve that did not require organ accompaniment, he dashed off some words and gave it to his organist, Franz

Gruber. Gruber, who also played the guitar, quickly composed a melody that could be accompanied by a few simple chords. From its first performance on that Christmas Eve till today, the quiet beauty of "Silent Night" has brought joy to millions of people.

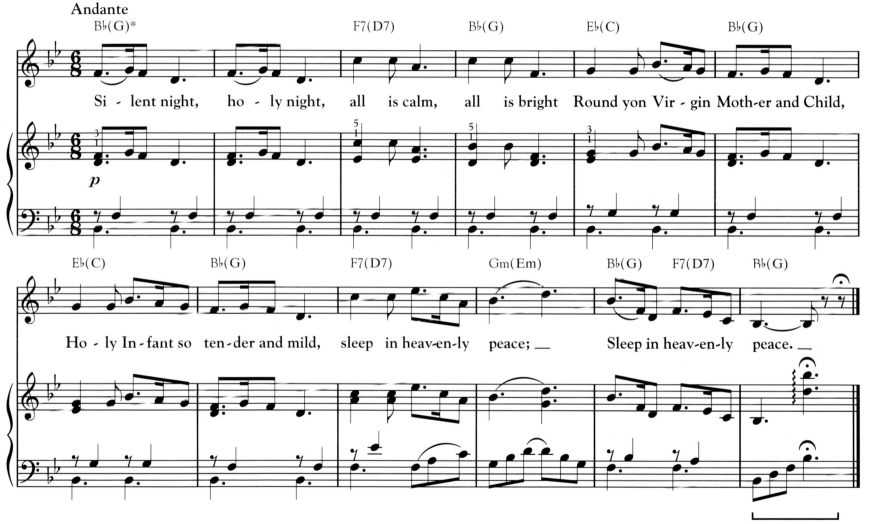

*Guitarists: Place capo on 3rd fret and use chord symbols in parentheses.

2. Silent night, holy night,
    Shepherds quake at the sight.
    Glories stream from heaven afar,
    Heav'nly hosts sing Alleluia;
    Christ, the Savior is born;
    Christ, the Savior is born.

3. Silent night, holy night,
    Son of God, love's pure light;
    Radiant beams from Thy holy face,
    With the dawn of redeeming grace,
    Jesus, Lord, at Thy birth;
    Jesus, Lord, at Thy birth.

The Coventry Carol

Traditional

HEROD WAS THE EVIL KING of Judea at the time when Jesus was born. When Herod heard a prophecy that a Child was born who would grow up to be the king of the Jews, he was overcome by fear of losing his power. The king sent his troops to find and kill all children under the age of two.

In a sixteenth-century English pageant that tells this story, the women of Bethlehem sing this carol as they lull their babies to sleep just before the soldiers come. The name of the carol comes from the town of Coventry where the pageant was performed.

By   by   lul - ly   lul - lay. _____

2. O sisters too, how may we do
   For to preserve this day
   This poor Youngling for whom we sing
   By, by, lully, lullay.

3. Herod, the king, in his raging
   Chargèd he hath this day
   His men of might in his own sight
   All children young to slay.

4. Then woe is me, poor Child, for Thee
   And ever morn and day
   For Thy parting, nor say, nor sing,
   By, by, lully, lullay.

Desmond Chute
English
Virgin and Child
Woodcut, 8.5 x 6 cm.
1924.93.13
© The Art Institute of Chicago

It Came Upon The Midnight Clear

Words by Edmund Hamilton Sears

Music by Richard S. Willis

UNITARIAN MINISTER Edmund Hamilton Sears wrote the deeply felt words of this hymn in 1849. Sears had a vision of an era of world peace (the "Age of Gold" mentioned in the fifth stanza) that could only be attained through the coming of Christ.

The hymn is often sung to a tune by Arthur Sullivan (of Gilbert and Sullivan fame), but the melody more familiar to Americans is called, appropriately enough, "Carol." It was adapted from a musical study by Richard S. Willis (1819–1900), a Boston-born composer and writer.

*Guitarists: Place capo on 3rd fret and play from chord symbols in parentheses.

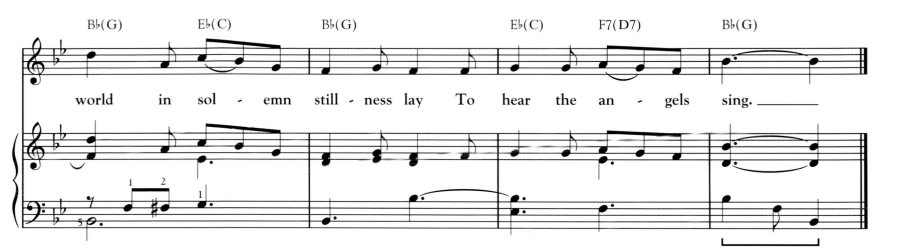

world in sol - emn still - ness lay To hear the an - gels sing. _____

2. Still through the cloven skies they come With peaceful wings unfurled,
   And still their heavenly music floats O'er all the weary world:
   Above its sad and lowly plains They bend on hovering wing,
   And ever o'er its Babel sounds The blessed angels sing.

3. Yet with the woes of sin and strife The world has suffered long;
   Beneath the heavenly strain have rolled Two-thousand years of wrong;
   And man, at war with man, hears not The tidings which they bring;
   O hush the noise, ye men of strife, And hear the angels sing.

4. O ye, beneath life's crushing load, Whose forms are bending low,
   Who toil along the climbing way With painful steps and slow,
   Look now! for glad and golden hours Come swiftly on the wing;
   O rest beside the weary road And hear the angels sing!

5. For lo! the days are hastening on, By prophet bards foretold,
   When with the ever-circling years Comes round the age of gold;
   When peace shall over all the earth Its ancient splendors fling,
   And the whole world send back the song Which now the angels sing.

Jolly Old St. Nicholas

Traditional

THE ORIGINAL SAINT NICHOLAS was a bishop in Asia Minor (present-day Turkey) in the fourth century A.D. Many stories were told about his miraculous powers. During a famine he convinced sailors of ships filled with grain to give his town enough to feed the people for two years. Nicholas promised that if they did this the sailors would find their ships filled with the original amounts of grain when they reached their home ports. Sure enough, the miracle was fulfilled and the sailors became the first converts of Saint Nicholas. He died in 342 A.D., and during the next fifteen hundred years he became the patron saint of many countries, including the Netherlands, where he was known as *Sant Nikolaas*. The Dutch brought the traditions associated with him—reindeer, flying sled, and presents for good children—to the New World and especially to New York, which was a Dutch colony until 1664.

Jol - ly old Saint Nich - o - las, lean your ear this way,
When the clock is strik - ing twelve and I'm fast a - sleep,

Don't you tell a sin - gle soul what I'm goin' to say.
Down the chim - ney broad and black with your pack you'll creep.

Christ - mas Eve is com - ing soon, now you dear old man,
All the stock - ings you will find hang - ing in a row,

Whis - per what you'll bring to me, tell me if you can.
Mine will be the short - est one, you'll be sure to know.

O Holy Night

Words by John Sullivan Dwight

(CANTIQUE DE NOËL)

Music by Adolphe-Charles Adam

FROM HIS EARLIEST YEARS Adolphe-Charles Adam wanted to be a composer. His father was a famous pianist and professor of music but did not want his son to become a musician. Adolphe decided to study in secret, finding instruction wherever and whenever he could. When the father finally found out about the study, he was angry. Yet, realizing the boy's talent and tenacity, he grudgingly allowed him to enter the conservatory on one condition: Adolphe had to promise *never* to write for the stage. Later, after Adam became France's most famous composer of comic operas, his father forgave him.

Today Adolphe-Charles Adam is chiefly remembered for his charming ballet, *Giselle*, and "Cantique de Noël" (Christmas Song), which we call "O Holy Night." The English words were written by John Sullivan Dwight (1818–1893), a Boston music teacher and critic.

Slowly, in 2 (each ♩. = 1 beat)

O ho - ly night! _____ The stars are bright - ly shin - ing, It is the night of the dear Sav - ior's birth. _____ Long lay the

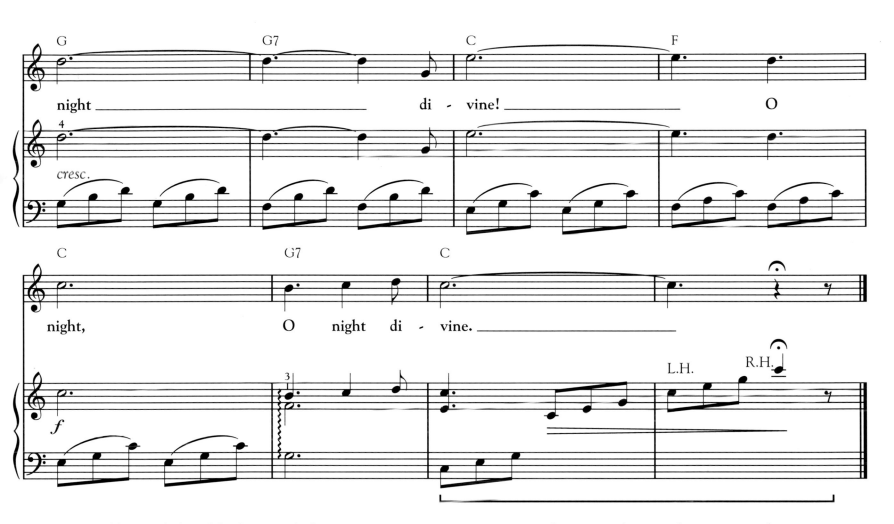

night _____ di - vine! _____ O

night, O night di - vine. _____

2. Led by the light of faith serenely beaming,
With glowing hearts by His cradle we stand;
So, led by light of a star sweetly gleaming,
Here came the wise men from the Orient land.
The King of Kings lay thus in lowly manger,
In all our trials born to be our friend;
He knows our need, to our weakness no stranger;
Behold your King! before him lowly bend!
Behold your King! your King before Him bend!

3. Truly He taught us to love one another;
His law is love and His Gospel is Peace.
Chains shall He break, for the slave is our brother,
And in His name all oppression shall cease.
Sweet hymns of joy in grateful chorus raise we,
Let all within us praise His holy Name.
Christ is the Lord, then ever, ever praise we
His pow'r and glory evermore proclaim,
His pow'r and glory evermore proclaim.

Christ Was Born On Christmas Day

Traditional

IN THE EARLY YEARS of Christianity, Christmas was celebrated on various days in December, January, or March. Then in the fifth century the Church decreed that Christmas ("Mass of Christ") would be celebrated on December 25. In some countries, such as Armenia, the birth of Jesus is celebrated on January 6, the day of his baptism, which is called Epiphany.

We Wish You A Merry Christmas

Traditional

ENGLAND'S ESTABLISHMENT of a reliable, cheap postal service in 1839 encouraged the writing of letters and cards, especially Christmas cards. This cheerful custom became widespread in the 1840s, and has lasted up to the present day. The colorful cards often showed scenes of carolers, called *waits*, strolling snowy streets, singing for a bit of "figgy pudding" or "a cup of good cheer." This famous Christmas song was originally a waits carol. It comes from mid-nineteenth-century Victorian England, although its author and exact date of publication are unknown.

With spirit

Verse — F(D)* · Bb(G) · G7(E7) · C7(A7)

We wish you a Mer-ry Christ-mas, We wish you a Mer-ry Christ-mas, We

F(D) · F7(D7) · Bb(G) · F(D) · Gm(Em) · C7(A7) · F(D) *Fine**

wish you a Mer-ry Christ-mas and a Hap-py New Year.

Chorus — F(D) · C(A) · Bb(G) · F(D) · C(A)

Good tid-ings to you wher-ev-er you are, Good

*Guitarists: Place capo on third fret and play from chord symbols in parentheses.
**Last time end here.

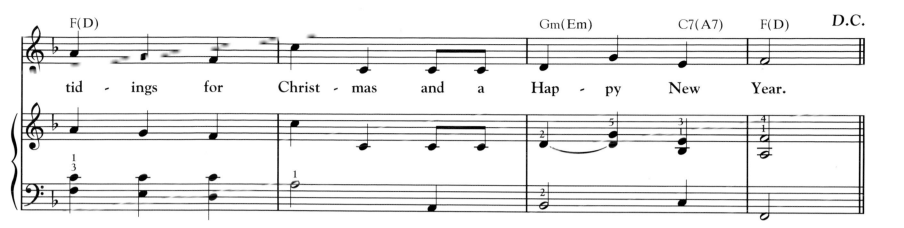

F(D)   Gm(Em)   C7(A7)   F(D)   *D.C.*

tid - ings   for   Christ - mas   and   a   Hap - py   New   Year.

2. Oh, bring us a figgy pudding,
   Oh, bring us a figgy pudding,
   Oh, bring us a figgy pudding,
   And a cup of good cheer.
   (repeat Chorus)

3. We won't go until we've got some,
   We won't go until we've got some,
   We won't go until we've got some,
   So bring some out here.
   (repeat Chorus)

4. We wish you a Merry Christmas,
   We wish you a Merry Christmas,
   We wish you a Merry Christmas,
   And a Happy New Year.

Doris Lee
American, 1905–1983
Thanksgiving, 1935
Oil on canvas, 71.4 x 101.6 cm.
Mr. and Mrs. Frank G. Logan Prize Fund,
1935.313
© The Art Institute of Chicago

Hark! The Herald Angels Sing

Words by Charles Wesley

Music by Felix Mendelssohn

FELIX MENDELSSOHN was only seventeen when his delightful overture to Shakespeare's *A Midsummer Night's Dream* established him as a genius in the musical world of Europe. Mendelssohn went on to write a large body of wonderful music in his short life of thirty-eight years. Symphonies, concertos, songs, and piano and chamber music flowed from his pen at an astonishing rate. In 1840 he composed a set of choral pieces for a festival that celebrated the invention of printing. The music of the second part of this was later adapted to words by Charles Wesley, brother of the man who founded Methodism. The hymn became a great favorite in England and in the United States even though Mendelssohn himself thought that the music was not suitable for a sacred text.

With th'an - gel - ic host pro - claim, Christ is ___ born in Beth - le - hem.

Hark! the her - ald an - gels sing Glo - ry ___ to the new - born King.

2. Christ, by highest heav'n adored,
   Christ the everlasting Lord,
   Late in time behold Him come,
   Offspring of a Virgin's womb!
   Veiled in flesh the Godhead see;
   Hail th'incarnate Deity!
   Pleased as Man with men to dwell,
   Jesus, our Immanuel.
   Hark! the herald angels sing,
   Glory to the new-born King.

3. Hail the heav'n born Prince of Peace!
   Hail the Sun of Righteousness!
   Light and life to all He brings,
   Ris'n with healing in His wings.
   Mild He lays His glory by,
   Born that man no more may die,
   Born to raise the sons of earth,
   Born to give them second birth.
   Hark! the herald angels sing,
   Glory to the new-born King.

Away In A Manger

Words: Unknown

Music (probably) by James R. Murray

MURRAY FIRST PUBLISHED this carol in his *Dainty Songs for Little Lads and Lasses, for use in the Kindergarten* in 1887. In this book he calls the song "Luther's Cradle Hymn" (composed by Martin Luther for his children, and still sung by German mothers to their little ones). However there is no evidence that the carol is by Luther. In fact, the words appeared anonymously in an earlier Lutheran publication, *Little Children's Book: for Schools and Families* and authorities feel that Murray himself wrote the music.

lit - tle Lord Je - sus a - sleep on the hay.

2. The cattle are lowing, the poor Baby wakes,
   But little Lord Jesus no crying He makes.
   I love Thee, Lord Jesus, look down from the sky,
   And stay by my cradle till morning is nigh.

3. Be near me, Lord Jesus, I ask Thee to stay
   Close by me forever and love me, I pray.
   Bless all the dear children in Thy tender care,
   And take us to heaven to live with Thee there.

Anonymous
German
The Nativity from *The Spice Garden of the Soul*, 1483
Woodcut, 7³/4 x 5 in.
Gift of Mrs. Potter Palmer Jr., 1947.438
© The Art Institute of Chicago

Good Christian Men, Rejoice

Words by John Mason Neale

Music: Anonymous

JOHN MASON NEALE (1818–1866) was an English minister who loved music. After illness forced him to retire from the ministry, he began collecting old hymns and translating them into English. These words are Neale's translation and adaptation of the Latin hymn *In dulci jubilo* (in sweet jubilation). The music is adapted from a fourteenth-century German melody.

Good Chris-tian men, re-joice, _____ With heart and soul and voice; _____

Give ye heed to what we say: Je-sus Christ is born to-day.

Ox and ass be-fore Him bow, And He is in the man-ger now.

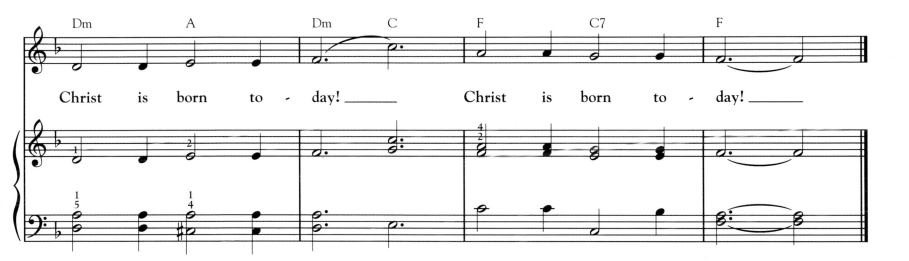

Christ is born to - day! _____ Christ is born to - day! _____

2. Good Christian men, rejoice,
   With heart and soul and voice;
   Now ye hear of endless bliss,
   Jesus Christ was born for this!
   He has op'ed the heav'nly door
   And man is blessed evermore.
   Christ was born for this!
   Christ was born for this!

3. Good Christian men, rejoice,
   With heart and soul and voice;
   Now ye need not fear the grave;
   Jesus Christ is born to save.
   Calls you one and calls you all,
   To gain His everlasting hall.
   Christ was born to save!
   Christ was born to save!

Lucas Cranach the Elder
German, 1472–1553
Angel from *The Wittenberg Book of Reliquaries*, 1509
Woodcut, 7⁵/8 x 5¹/2 in.
Clarence Buckingham Collection, 1948.111
© The Art Institute of Chicago

Angels We Have Heard On High

Traditional

ONE OF THE MOST POPULAR carols of all time, this comes from several sources, authors unknown. It is actually a combination of three different songs. The music of the first part comes from an eighteenth-century popular song. The words are a translation of a French carol, "Les Anges dans nos Campagnes" (Angels in our Countryside). The famous refrain, "Gloria in excelsis Deo," is thought to date back to medieval times. The carol was first published in its present form in 1855.

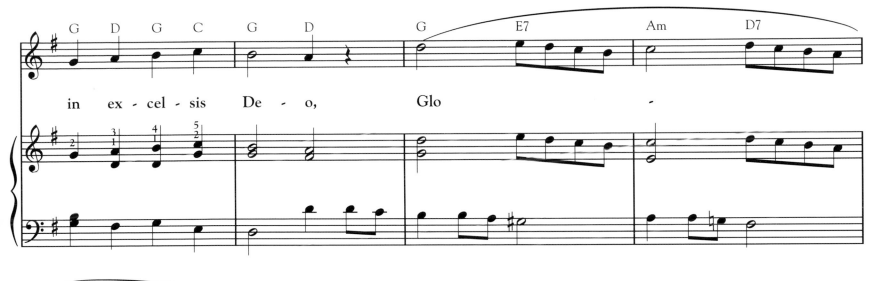

in ex - cel - sis De - o, Glo -

- ri - a in ex - cel - sis De - o.

2. Shepherds, why this jubilee?
   Why your joyous strains prolong?
   What the gladsome tidings be
   Which inspire your heav'nly song!
   (repeat Chorus)

3. Come to Bethlehem and see
   Him whose birth the angels sing.
   Come adore on bended knee
   Christ the Lord, the new-born King.
   (repeat Chorus)

The Boar's Head Carol

Traditional

THIS FIFTEENTH-CENTURY English carol was sung while the festive dish, consisting of a roasted boar's head decorated with flowers, herbs, and spices, was brought into the banquet. Although most people today would cringe at the thought, five hundred years ago boar's head was a traditional Christmas dish.

This carol is also an example of what is called macaronic verse, a poem in which English and Latin are mixed. Macaronic seems to be derived from the Italian *macaroni*, possibly because of the way pasta is mixed with sauce.

Here is the Latin in this carol, translated: *Caput apri defero* (I carry the boar's head); *Reddens laudes Domino* (Giving praises to God); *Qui estis in convivio* (You who are at the banquet).

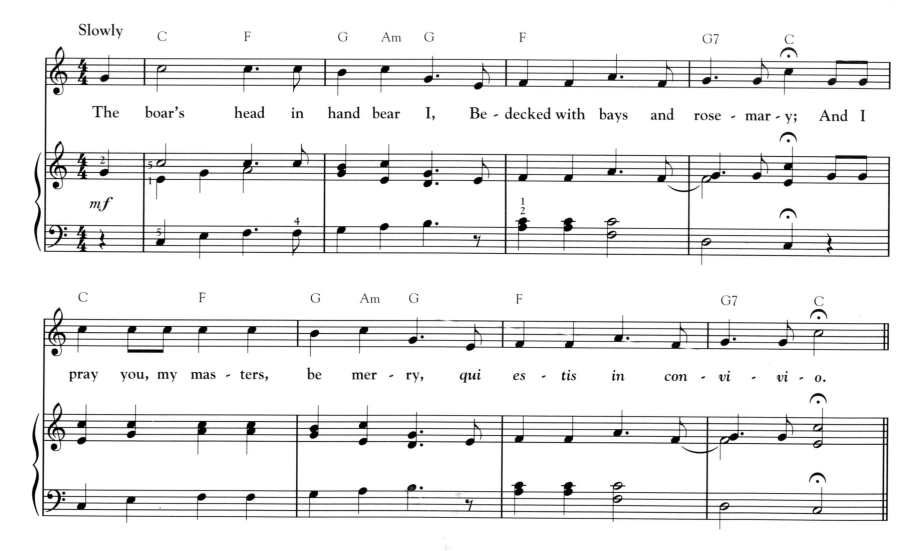

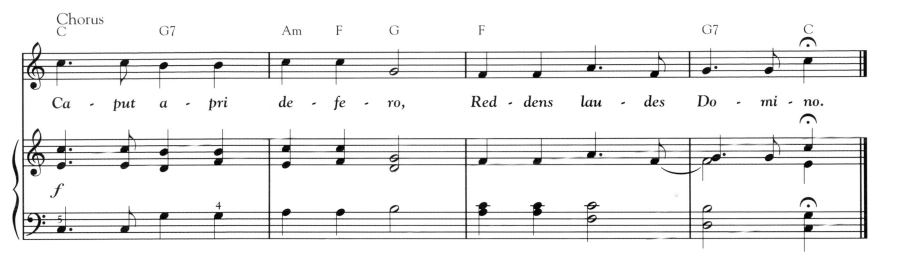

Chorus

Ca - put a - pri de - fe - ro, Red - dens lau - des Do - mi - no.

2. The boar's head, as I understand,
   Is the rarest dish in all the land
   Which thus bedecked with gay garland,
   Let us *servire cantico.*
       (Chorus)

3. Our steward hath provided this
   In honor of the King of bliss
   Which on this day to be served is
   In Reginensi atrio.
       (Chorus)

Panel from American
Album Quilt, 1845–1850
Cotton appliqued, embroidered and
quilted, 228 x 229.5 cm.
Mrs. Chauncey B. Borland, 1957.524
© The Art Institute of Chicago

Up On The Housetop

Traditional

AS EARLY AS the seventeenth century, Dutch boys and girls could expect a gift from Saint Nicholas at Christmas time—nice presents for the good children, but only switches for spanking for the naughty ones. The Dutch brought this custom to the New World, and when the English-speaking people heard the Dutch name for Saint Nicholas, Sant (Ni)kolaas, it sounded to them like Santa Claus. More important, the original rather stern, judgmental character of Saint Nicholas became softened to the more generous, forgiving Santa Claus

of today (although we still sing "He's . . . gonna find out who's naughty and nice").

One of the reasons we picture Santa as we do is C. C. Moore's famous 1822 poem, "A Visit from Saint Nicholas," also known as "'Twas the Night Before Christmas." In it we see Santa, his sleigh and reindeer, and his method of delivering Christmas presents. "Up On The Housetop" is an American song written a few years after Moore's poem became popular.

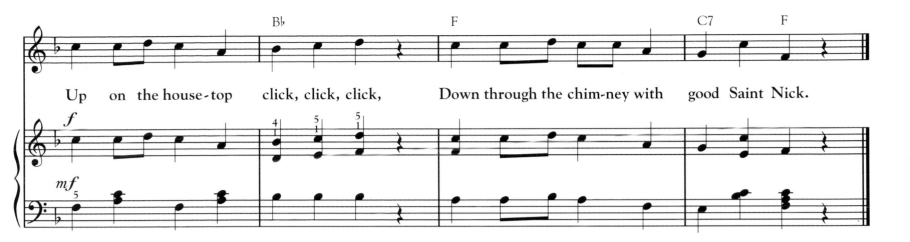

Up on the house-top click, click, click, Down through the chim-ney with good Saint Nick.

2. First comes the stocking of little Nell;
Oh, dear Santa, fill it well!
Give her a dolly that laughs and cries,
One that opens and shuts her eyes.
(repeat Chorus)

3. Next comes the stocking of little Bill;
Oh, just see that glorious fill!
There's a hammer and lots of tacks,
A choo-choo train with lots of tracks.
(repeat Chorus)

Here We Come A-Wassailing

(HERE WE COME A-CAROLING)
(THE WASSAIL SONG)

MANY YEARS AGO bands of musicians, called English waits, roved the streets during the holiday season, singing and playing carols like this one in the hopes of getting a few pennies, or some food or drink. "Wassail" was a drink made of ale or wine spiced with roasted apples and sugar. The name comes from an old Anglo-Saxon toast, "Waes Hael" (be healthy). Soon after the Angles and Saxons invaded Britain in the fifth and sixth centuries, they adopted Christianity and used "Waes Hael" as a toast to the Lord. And that's how wassail became associated with Christmas.

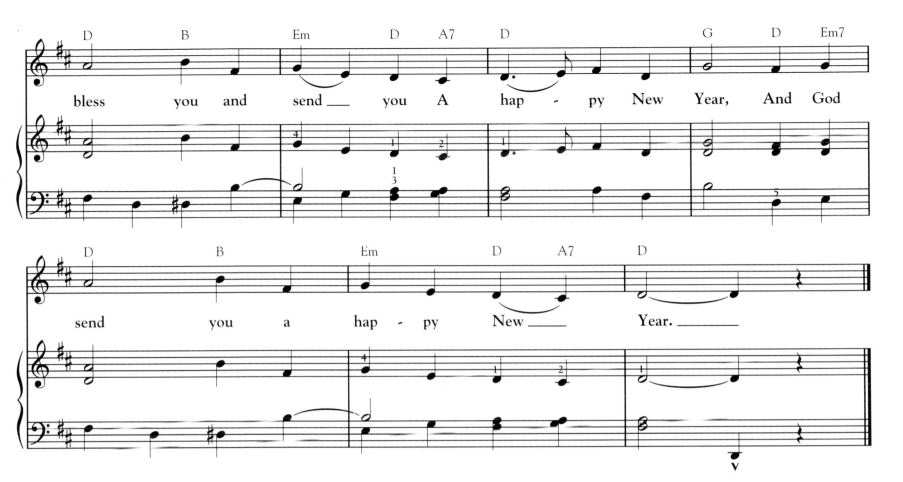

bless you and send ___ you A hap - py New Year, And God

send you a hap - py New ___ Year. ___

2. We <u>are</u> not daily beggars
   That beg from door to door,
   But we are neighbors' children
   Whom you have seen before.
     (repeat Chorus)

3. We have got a little purse
   Of stretching leather skin;
   We want a little of your money
   To line it well within.
     (repeat Chorus)

4. Bring us out a table,
   And spread it with a cloth;
   Bring us out a moldy cheese,
   And some of your Christmas loaf.
     (repeat Chorus)

5. God <u>bless</u> the master of this house,
   Likewise the mistress too;
   And all the little children
   That round the table go.
     (repeat Chorus)

Angels From The Realms Of Glory

Words by James Montgomery

Music by Henry Smart

YEARS BEFORE HE WROTE the words for this hymn, the young English clergyman James Montgomery was arrested. The arrest occurred soon after the American colonies had won their independence and while the French revolution was raging in Europe. Fearing that Montgomery's articles could stir up revolutionary sentiment in England, authorities put him in jail to prevent him from publishing further.

But he wrote anyway, and the resultant book was such a success that Montgomery went on to a long career as a writer and publisher. Henry Smart, who wrote the music, was an organist and composer who came from a famous family of English musicians. He lived from 1813 to 1879, but in about 1864 he went blind and had to compose all his music by dictating it to a secretary.

*Guitarists: Place capo on 2nd fret and use chord symbols in parentheses.

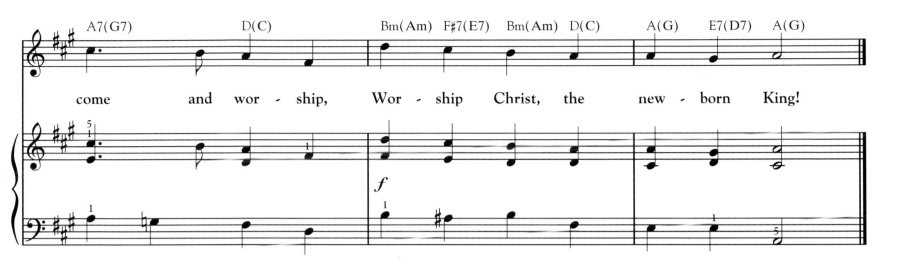

come and wor - ship, Wor - ship Christ, the new - born King!

2. Shepherds, in the fields abiding,
   Watching o'er your flocks by night,
   God with man is now residing,
   Yonder shines the Infant light.
   Come and worship, come and worship,
   Worship Christ, the new-born King!

3. Sages, leave your contemplations,
   Brighter visions beam afar;
   Seek the great desire of nations;
   Ye have seen His natal star.
   Come and worship, come and worship,
   Worship Christ, the new-born King!

4. Saints, before the altar bending,
   Watching long in hope and fear,
   Suddenly the Lord descending
   In his temple shall appear.
   Come and worship, come and worship,
   Worship Christ, the new-born King!

Colyn de Coter
Netherlandish, c. 1450/1455–before 1539/1540
Virgin and Child Crowned by Angels, 1490/1510
Oil on panel, 152.3 x 88.6 cm.
. and Mrs. Martin A. Ryerson Collection, 1933.1039
© The Art Institute of Chicago

Caroling, Caroling

Words by Wihla Hutson

Music by Alfred Burt

MOST OF THE CAROLS we know and love were written prior to the twentieth century. Some date back to the Middle Ages, more than a thousand years ago! Yet some twentieth-century carols carry on the tradition and bring a new feeling and fresh harmonies to the Christmas season.

Cases in point are the following two carols by American composer Alfred Burt. He graduated from the Michigan School of Music in 1942 and then served in the Army Air Force Band. After the war he joined various dance bands as

trumpet player and arranger. In the early forties he began writing Christmas carols, often with lyricist Wihla Hutson. At first these carols were meant only for family Christmas cards, but after Burt's tragic death in 1954 at the age of only thirty-three, his wife had the carols published. Since then these gems of modern writing have gradually gained acceptance and have been recorded by such stars as Nat Cole, Tony Bennett, Johnny Mathis, Harry Connick, Jr., and the Boston Pops under John Williams, to name just a few.

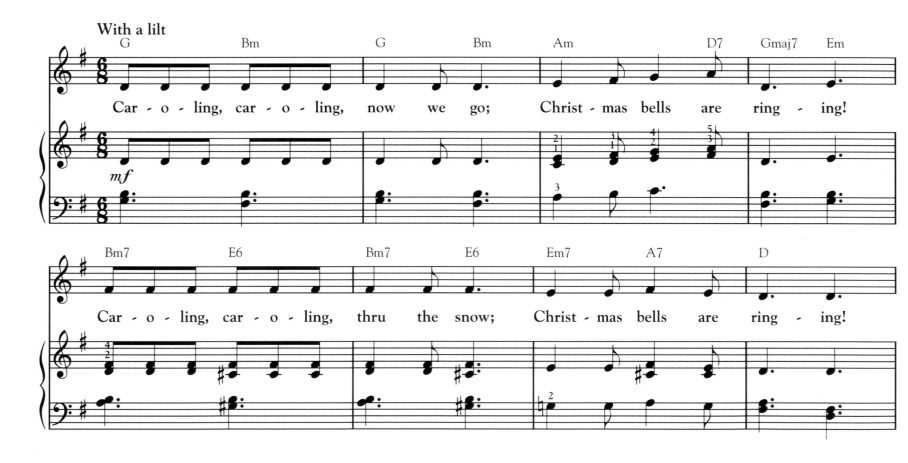

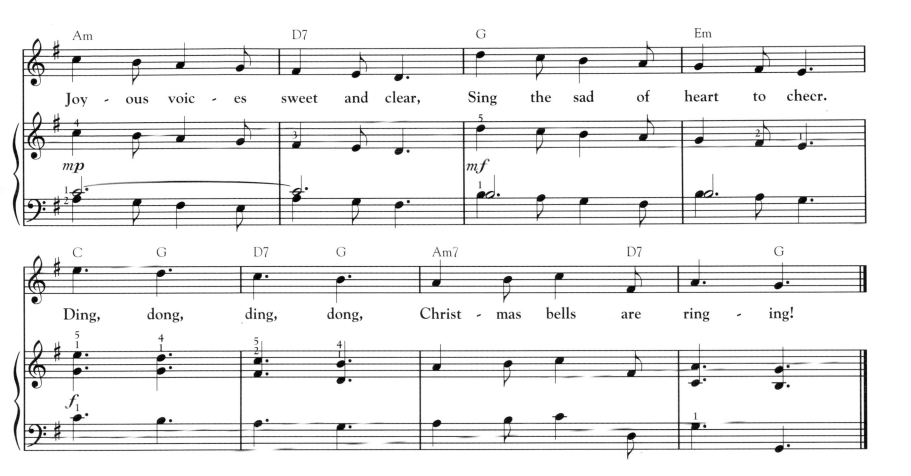

Joy - ous voic - es sweet and clear, Sing the sad of heart to cheer.

Ding, dong, ding, dong, Christ - mas bells are ring - ing!

2. Caroling, caroling, thru the town;
   Christmas bells are ringing!
   Caroling, caroling, up and down;
   Christmas bells are ringing!
   Mark ye well the song we sing,
   Gladsome tidings now we bring.
   Ding, dong, ding, dong,
   Christmas bells are ringing!

3. Caroling, caroling, near and far;
   Christmas bells are ringing!
   Following, following yonder star;
   Christmas bells are ringing!
   Sing we all this happy morn,
   "Lo, the King of heav'n is born!"
   Ding, dong, ding, dong,
   Christmas bells are ringing!

Julius Klinger
German
Flugplatz Berlin Johannisthal, 1908
Early 20th-century poster design
Ryerson Library Collection
© The Art Institute of Chicago

Some Children See Him

Words by Wihla Hutson

Music by Alfred Burt

chil - dren see Him bronzed and __ brown, With dark and heav - y __ hair.

2. Some children see Him almond eyed,
This Savior whom we kneel beside.
Some children see Him almond eyed,
With skin of yellow hue.
Some children see Him dark as they,
Sweet Mary's Son to whom we pray;
Some children see Him dark as they,
And ah! they love Him too!

3. The children in each diff'rent place
Will see the Baby Jesus' face
Like theirs, but bright with heav'nly grace
And filled with holy light.
O lay aside each earthly thing,
And with thy heart as offering,
Come worship now the Infant King,
'Tis love that's born tonight!

Edgar Miller
American, 1899–1993
Poster Stamp (Nativity), c. 1930
Adapted from *Die Gebrauchsgraphik*, 1930
Ryerson Library Collection
© The Art Institute of Chicago and Edgar Miller

Jingle Bells

Words and Music by James Pierpont

ALTHOUGH HE CAME from a famous family (he was the uncle of financier J. P. Morgan), James Pierpont was something of a rebel. Much to the horror of his abolitionist father, he took up the Confederate cause before the Civil War and even moved to the South. He wrote many songs but is remembered only for this one, arguably the best-known Christmas song in the world. But "Jingle Bells" started out as a Thanksgiving song! In 1857 it was published as "The One-Horse Open Sleigh," with the lyric printed here. In 1859 it was reissued as "Jingle Bells" and gradually attained the worldwide familiarity it enjoys today.

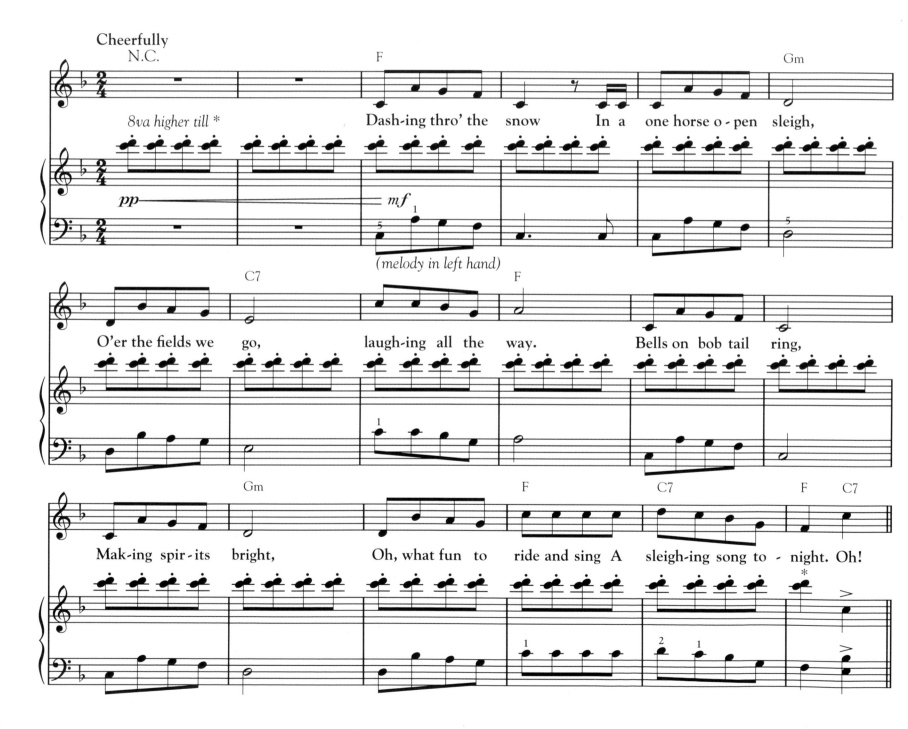

2. A day or two ago
   I thought I'd take a ride,
   And soon Miss Fannie Bright
   Was seated by my side.
   The horse was lean and lank;
   Misfortune seemed his lot.
   He got into a drifted bank
   And we, we got upsot.
       (repeat Chorus)

3. A day or two ago,
   The story I must tell:
   I went out on the snow
   And on my back I fell.
   A gent was riding by
   In a one-horse open sleigh,
   He laughed as there I sprawling lie,
   But quickly drove away.
       (repeat Chorus)

4. Now the ground is white;
   Go it while you're young.
   Take the girls tonight
   And sing this sleighing song.
   Just get a bobtailed bay,
   Two forty as his speed.
   Hitch him to an open sleigh
   And crack! You'll take the lead.
       (repeat Chorus)

Jesu, Joy Of Man's Desiring

Johann Sebastian Bach

THE MUSIC of the baroque period (about 1600 to 1750) was brought to its highest level by the towering figure of J. S. Bach. He was a master of all forms of composition, especially counterpoint, the art of combining two or more melodies to form a beautiful, ever-changing musical texture. As was common in that era, Bach borrowed from another composer's work, a 1642 hymn by Johann Schop, for the basis of his famous "Jesu, Joy of Man's Desiring." Bach's graceful flowing lines of eighth notes transformed the somewhat plain hymn into the masterpiece we know today. It is interesting to note that the title is not Bach's, but was added much later when the piece became popular in England and America. The English title comes from a poem by Robert Bridges (1844–1930), the British Poet Laureate.

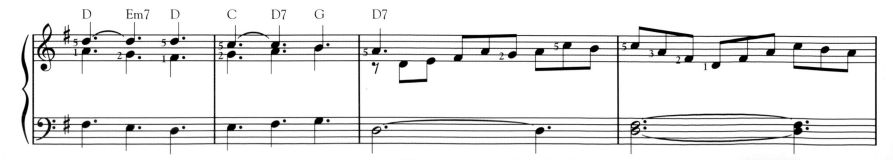

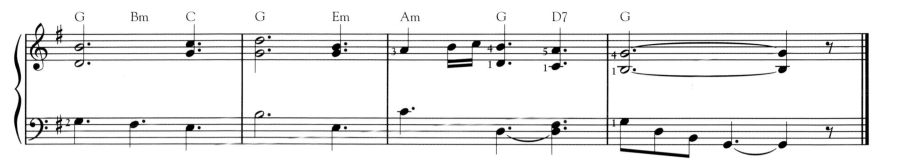

Desmond Chute
English
Christ Child with Animals
Woodcut, 9.4 x 11 cm.
1924.93.12
© The Art Institute of Chicago

Joy To The World

Words by Isaac Watts

Music by Lowell Mason

WHEN ISAAC WATTS was only eighteen, he complained to his minister father that the hymns they sang in church were of inferior quality. The deacon, a staunch upholder of tradition, angrily challenged Isaac to write a better one. By the next Sunday the young poet had produced the first of hundreds of beautiful lyrics that he would write in a life that lasted from 1674 to 1748. "Joy to the World" comes from his 1719 collection, *The Psalms of David, Imitated.*

Fully 120 years later, Lowell Mason, an American music teacher and composer, set the words to music. He called his tune "Antioch," and because two of its themes resembled parts of *The Messiah,* Mason gave credit to his idol, the great German/English composer, George Frederick Handel. But since most of the music is original with Mason, authorities now credit him as sole composer.

Majestically

sing, And heav'n and heav'n and na - ture sing.

2. Joy to the earth! the Savior reigns;
   Let men their songs employ;
   While fields and floods, rocks, hills and plains,
   Repeat the sounding joy.

3. No more let sins and sorrows grow,
   Nor thorns infest the ground;
   He comes to make His blessings flow
   Far as the curse is found.

4. He rules the world with truth and grace;
   And makes the nations prove
   The glories of His righteousness,
   And wonders of His love.

Good King Wenceslas

Words by John Mason Neale   *Music: Anonymous*

WENCESLAS WAS a real king! Over one thousand years ago he ruled over the land of Bohemia, part of what is today the Czech Republic in central Europe. During his reign Wenceslas earned a reputation for kindness and generosity, but he came to a violent end in 929, murdered by a jealous younger brother.

In 1853 John Mason Neale (see "Good Christian Men, Rejoice") was given a copy of an ancient collection of church and school songs. In it he found a thirteenth-century Latin song called *Tempus adest floridum* ("Spring has unfolded her flowers"). He wrote new words to this melody and in 1854 published the result, the carol we know as "Good King Wenceslas."

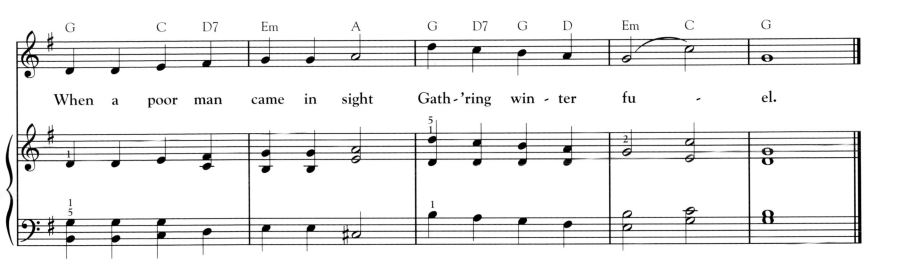

When a poor man came in sight Gath-'ring win-ter fu - el.

2. "Hither, page, and stand by me,
   If thou know'st it, telling,
   Yonder peasant, who is he?
   Where and what his dwelling?"
   "Sire, he lives a good league hence,
   Underneath the mountain,
   Right against the forest fence,
   By Saint Agnes' fountain."

3. "Bring me flesh, and bring me wine,
   Bring me pine logs hither:
   Thou and I will see him dine,
   When we bear them thither."
   Page and monarch, forth they went,
   Forth they went together
   Through the rude wind's wild lament
   And the bitter weather.

4. "Sire, the night is darker now,
   And the wind blows stronger;
   Fails my heart, I know not how;
   I can go no longer."
   "Mark my footsteps, good my page,
   Tread thou in them boldly;
   Thou shalt find the winter's rage
   Freeze thy blood less coldly."

5. In his master's steps he trod,
   Where the snow lay dinted;
   Heat was in the very sod
   Which the Saint had printed.
   Therefore, Christian men, be sure,
   Wealth or rank possessing,
   Ye who now will bless the poor,
   Shall yourselves find blessing.

We Three Kings Of Orient Are

Words and Music by John Henry Hopkins

AMERICAN MINISTER John Henry Hopkins wrote this carol for a Christmas pageant in 1857. At that time he was criticized for calling the Wise Men "kings." The Bible mentions only "men from the East." Nevertheless, the carol has survived for well over a century without losing popularity.

The three kings are Melchior, who brings gold to crown the new King; Gaspar, who brings frankincense, an aromatic gum used to make incense, to praise the King; and Balthazar, whose gift of myrrh (an aromatic gum used in burials) foretells the death of Jesus on the cross.

Melchior

2. Born a King on Bethlehem's plain,
Gold I bring, to crown him again,
King for ever, ceasing never
Over us all to reign.
    (repeat Chorus)

Gaspar

3. Frankincense to offer have I,
Incense owns a Deity nigh.
Prayer and praising, all men raising
Worship Him, God most high.
    (repeat Chorus)

Balthazar

4. Myrrh is mine, its bitter perfume
Breathes a life of gathering gloom;
Sorrowing, sighing, bleeding, dying,
Sealed in the stone-cold tomb.
    (repeat Chorus)

5. Glorious now behold Him arise,
King and God and Sacrifice;
Alleluia, Alleluia!
Sounds through the earth and skies.
    (repeat Chorus)

O Christmas Tree

(O Tannenbaum)

Traditional

DECORATING A CHRISTMAS TREE at holiday time was originally a German custom, but in the last two hundred years or so the custom has spread all over the world. Possibly because Christmas comes around the same time as the Jewish Festival of Lights (Hanukkah) we, too, decorate our trees with lights.

The melody for this carol is that of a German folk song first published in 1799. There have been many different sets of words for this tune, including the college song "Lauriger Horatius," and the great rallying song of the Confederacy, "Maryland, My Maryland." Yet it is as a hymn in praise of the beloved Christmas tree that the song remains popular.

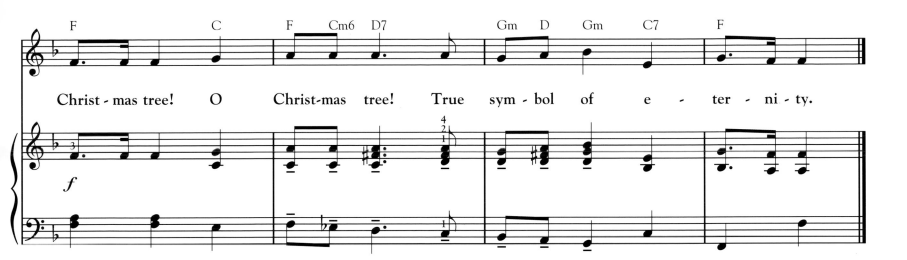

Christ - mas tree! O Christ-mas tree! True sym - bol of e - ter - ni - ty.

2. O Christmas Tree! O Christmas tree!
   You fill all hearts with gaiety.
   O Christmas tree! O Christmas tree!
   You fill all hearts with gaiety.
   On Christmas Day you stand so tall,
   Affording joy to one and all.
   O Christmas tree! O Christmas tree!
   You fill all hearts with gaiety.

3. O Christmas tree! O Christmas tree!
   Your candles glow delightfully.
   O Christmas tree! O Christmas tree!
   Your candles glow delightfully.
   Their flick'ring flames send forth a light,
   Like twinkling stars that shine at night.
   O Christmas tree! O Christmas tree!
   Your candles glow delightfully.

Panel from American *Album Quilt*,
1845–1850
Cotton appliqued, embroidered and
quilted, 228 x 229.5 cm.
Mrs. Chauncey B. Borland, 1957.524
© The Art Institute of Chicago

Go Tell It On The Mountain

Traditional

UNTIL THE CIVIL WAR, white America had pretty much ignored African-American music. During that conflict, several white officers of black regiments wrote down the melodies they heard their soldiers singing. The first collection of these songs was published in 1867. Shortly after that, an African-American choral group called the Fisk University Jubilee Singers made many of these melodies, now called spirituals, widely known.

The story of Jesus was very appealing to the slaves. In his struggle to set men free they saw a parallel with their own aspirations toward freedom. So the birth of Jesus described in this spiritual also represented the birth of hope for freedom from slavery.

*Guitarists: Place capo on 3rd fret and use chord symbols in parentheses

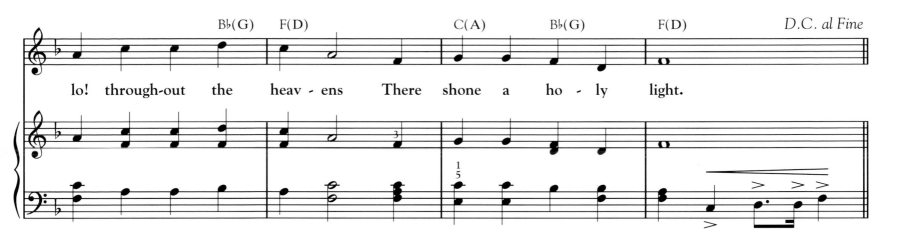

D.C. al Fine

lo! through-out the heav - ens There shone a ho - ly light.

2. The shepherds feared and trembled
   When high above the earth
   Rang out an angel chorus
   To hail our Savior's birth.
        (repeat Chorus)

3. And lo! when they had heard it
   They all bowed down to pray
   And traveled on together
   To where the Baby lay.
        (repeat Chorus)

Anonymous Book of Hours
French
The Annunciation of the Shepherds, c. 1470
Illumination on vellum, 16.5 x 10.2 cm.
Gift of Sarah Raymond Fitzwilliam, 1917.796
© The Art Institute of Chicago

The Twelve Days Of Christmas

Traditional

THE TWELVE DAYS OF CHRISTMAS stretch from Christmas Day to Epiphany on January 6. The custom of gift-giving arose from the first Epiphany, when the Wise Men brought gifts to the infant Jesus. During the Middle Ages, Christmas gift-giving among the nobility had become an elaborate affair, as this carol tells us.

"The Twelve Days of Christmas" is called a "cumulative carol." This means that each new verse adds another item such as a gift, until the twelfth verse has all twelve. In olden times children made a game of this. Each child had to sing the carol from memory, and the child who forgot a gift had to pay a penalty.

Although this carol wasn't published until 1868, it was sung at least three hundred years earlier.

*Guitarists: Place capo on 3rd fret and play from chord symbols in parentheses.

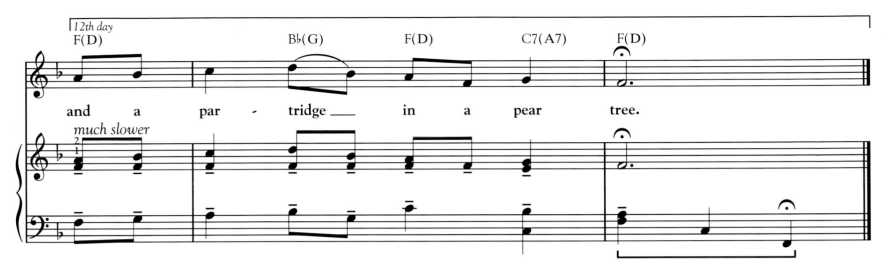

Performance note: For the seventh to twelfth day play from the sign 𝄋 repeating the marked measure as often as necessary.

7. On the seventh day of Christmas my true love sent to me
seven swans a-swimming, six geese a-laying, five golden rings,
four calling birds, three French hens, two turtledoves,
and a partridge in a pear tree.

8. On the eighth day of christmas my true love sent to me
eight maids a-milking, seven swans a-swimming, etc.

9. On the ninth day of Christmas my true love sent to me
nine ladies dancing, eight maids a-milking, etc.

10. On the tenth day of Christmas my true love sent to me
ten lords a-leaping, nine ladies dancing, etc.

11. On the eleventh day of Christmas my true love sent to me
eleven pipers piping, ten lords a-leaping, etc.

12. On the twelfth day of Christmas my true love sent to me
twelve drummers drumming, eleven pipers piping,
ten lords a-leaping, nine ladies dancing,
eight maids a-milking, seven swans a-swimming,
six gesse a-laying, five golden rings,
four calling birds, three French hens,
two turtledoves, and a partridge in a pear tree.

H. Giacomelli
French
The Bird Perch, color plate
Adapted from *French Illustrators*, 1895
Part I
Ryerson Library Collection
© The Art Institute of Chicago

O Come, O Come, Emmanuel

Traditional

MILLIONS OF PEOPLE and especially those of the Catholic faith revere the serenely beautiful melodies called Gregorian chants. Originally called Latin plainsong, these chants date back before music had harmony (accompanying chords) or measured notation (a steady beat). Plainsong was already old when Pope (later Saint) Gregory had hundreds of them written down in the late sixth and early seventh centuries. In his honor we call them Gregorian chants.

The music of this carol is thought to date back to the time of Gregory, but through the years writers and arrangers have added harmony, measured notation, and a lovely set of English words. Emmanuel, a poetic name for Jesus, comes from the Hebrew "God is with us." "Rod of Jesse" means that Jesus came from the tribe of Jesse.

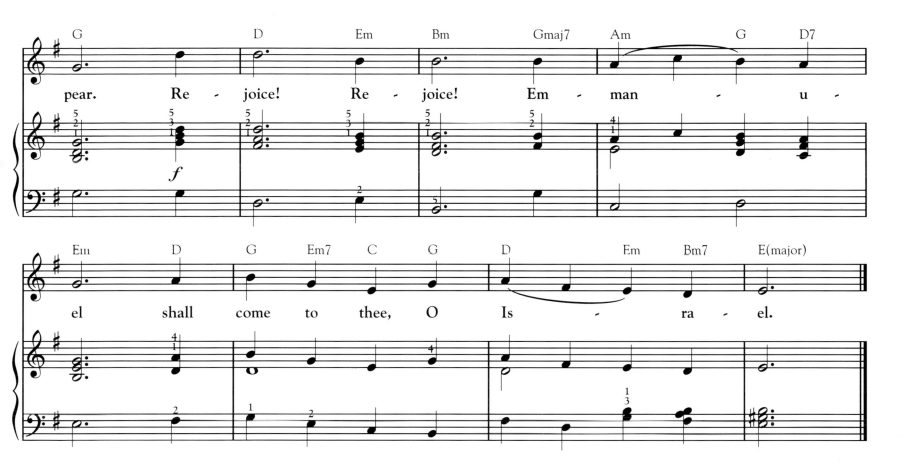

pear. Re - joice! Re - joice! Em - man - u - el shall come to thee, O Is - ra - el.

2. O come, Thou Rod of Jesse, free
   Thine own from Satan's tyranny;
   From depths of hell Thy people save
   And give them vict'ry o'er the grave.
   (repeat Chorus)

3. O come Thou dayspring, come and cheer
   Our spirits by Thine advent here;
   And drive away the shades of night,
   And pierce the clouds and bring us light.
   (repeat Chorus)

Deck The Halls

Traditional

BEFORE CHRISTIANITY REACHED BRITAIN, pagan tribes had long been decorating their dwellings with holly boughs as protection against witches and evil spirits. With the arrival of Christianity this tradition continued, and we still think of red and green (the bright berries and dark leaves of the holly) as the colors of Christmas.

The melody of this well-loved carol is Welsh. The original Welsh words were not about Christmas, but were instead about New Year's night. The familiar words printed here are American and date from the 1880s.

Troll the an - cient Yule - tide car - ol, Fa la la la la la la la la.

2. See the blazing Yule before us,
   Fa la la la la la la la la.
   Strike the harp and join the chorus,
   Fa la la la la la la la la.
   Follow me in merry measure
   Fa la la la la la la
   While I tell of Yuletide treasure,
   Fa la la la la la la la la.

3. Fast away the old year passes
   Fa la la la la la la la la.
   Hail the new, ye lads and lasses,
   Fa la la la la la la la la.
   Sing we joyous all together,
   Fa la la la la la la
   Heedless of the wind and weather,
   Fa la la la la la la la la.

Panel from American
Album Quilt, 1845–1850
Cotton appliqued, embroidered
and quilted, 228 x 229.5 cm.
Mrs. Chauncey B. Borland, 1957.524
© The Art Institute of Chicago

All Through The Night

Traditional

No ONE KNOWS WHO WROTE this beautiful carol. It was first published in the late eighteenth century in England in translation from a book called *Musical* and *Poetical Relicks of the Welsh Bards*. Since then the original poem has been translated and modified many different times. This version is the best known.

*Guitarists: Place capo on 3rd fret and play from chord symbols in parentheses.

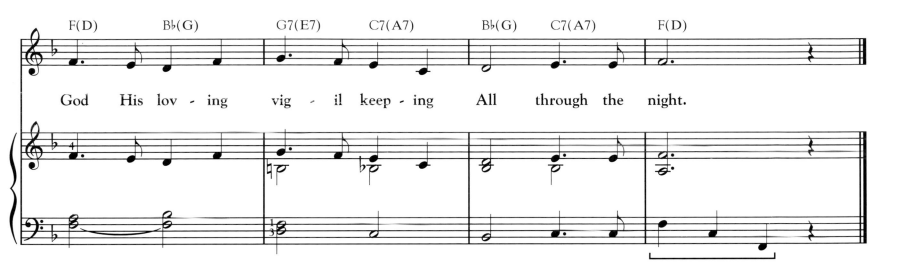

God His lov- ing vig - il keep- ing All through the night.

2. While the moon her watch is keeping
   All through the night;
   While the weary world is sleeping
   All through the night.
   Through your dreams you're swiftly stealing,
   Visions of delight revealing,
   Christmas time is so appealing
   All through the night.

3. You, my God, a Babe of wonder
   All through the night;
   Dreams you dream can't break from thunder
   All through the night.
   Children's dreams cannot be broken,
   Life is but a lovely token.
   Christmas should be softly spoken
   All through the night.

Peter Paul Rubens
Flemish, 1577–1640
Detail from *The Adoration of the Eucharist,* c. 1626
Oil on panel, 32.1 x 31.8 cm.
Mr. and Mrs. Martin A. Ryerson Collection,
1937.1012
© The Art Institute of Chicago

Index

Jacob Cornelisz. van Amsterdam
(also van Oostsanen)
Netherlandish, c. 1470–1533
Detail from *Adoration of the Christ Child*, c. 1520
Oil on panel, 98.7 x 76.5 cm.
George F. Harding Collection, 1983.375
© The Art Institute of Chicago